EYEWITNESS TO
JAPANESE
INTERNMENT

BY JILL ROESLER

Published by The Child's World®
1980 Lookout Drive • Mankato, MN 56003-1705
800-599-READ • www.childsworld.com

Acknowledgments
The Child's World®: Mary Berendes, Publishing Director
Red Line Editorial: Design, editorial direction, and production
Photographs ©: Bettmann/Corbis, cover, 1; Everett Historical/Shutterstock Images, 4,
6, 10, 16, 23; Red Line Editorial, 7; Kyodo/AP Images, 9; Corbis, 13, 24; Ansel Adams/
Library of Congress, 14; Tom Grundy/Shutterstock Images, 19; Horace Cort/AP
Images, 20; The Mariners' Museum/Corbis, 26; Dennis Cook/AP Images, 29

ISBN 9781634074131

LCCN 2015946227

Printed in the United States of America
Mankato, MN
December, 2015
PA02281

ABOUT THE AUTHOR
Jill Roesler is from southern Minnesota. In addition to writing children's
books, she writes for several newspapers. Her favorite subject to research
and write about is history. In her free time, Roesler enjoys reading, traveling,
and gardening.

TABLE OF
CONTENTS

Chapter 1

ATTACK ON PEARL HARBOR

On December 7, 1941, Asako Tokuno stood on a street corner in California. She was waiting for the bus to her university. It was the week of final exams. But Tokuno was not thinking about her tests. She felt uneasy. Tokuno was a Japanese-American woman. She had never felt that her **ethnicity** mattered. But now it did.

◄ The bombing of Pearl Harbor, Hawaii, began a war between the United States and Japan.

"As I'd stand on that corner, I would get this terrible feeling that people were watching, looking at me," Tokuno said.[1]

Earlier that day, Japanese forces had launched a surprise attack on the United States. Fighter planes dropped bombs on the U.S. Navy base at Pearl Harbor, Hawaii. The attack damaged battleships and planes. It left more than 2,400 Americans dead. The next day, President Franklin D. Roosevelt asked Congress to declare war on Japan. Three days later, Italy and Germany declared war on the United States. Italy and Germany were Japan's **allies**. The United States had entered World War II.

After the attack, Americans worried about their safety. Many felt **prejudice** against Japanese immigrants. They believed that the immigrants were not loyal to the United States. Some suspected the immigrants of spying on the United States for Japan. The children of Japanese immigrants also faced prejudice, even though they were born in the United States. Some had never even seen Japan.

Asako Tokuno grew up in Richmond, California. Her parents had immigrated to the United States before she was born. Many Japanese Americans lived in their city. Between 1886 and 1911, thousands of Japanese immigrants had sailed to the United

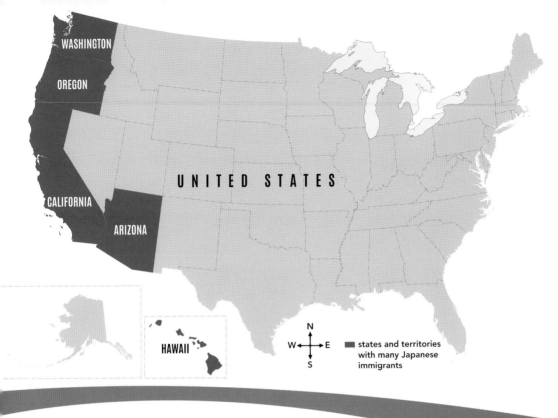

▲ Many Japanese immigrants moved to western states or territories such as Arizona, California, Hawaii, Oregon, and Washington.

States. Most were looking for jobs. More than 400,000 settled along the West Coast. Japanese people continued to immigrate to the United States in the 1920s and 1930s. The immigrants were called *Issei*, which means "first generation" in Japanese. Tokuno's parents opened a successful flower shop. Other Issei workers found jobs as miners, farmers, and loggers. Eventually, many opened their own businesses.

◄ After the attack on Pearl Harbor, a Japanese-American man put up a sign on his grocery store.

Most of the immigrants' children grew up with Japanese traditions. But they also learned American ways of life. They were called *Nisei*, or "second generation." Many Nisei children lived in two different worlds. They usually spoke English in public. But they often spoke Japanese at home. Nisei were American-born citizens. Most Nisei wanted to be known as Japanese Americans, not as Japanese people who lived in the United States.

But after the Pearl Harbor attack, everything changed. Tokuno later described her experiences. Four years after the bombing, she lived with her sister in an apartment building in St. Paul, Minnesota. "Our landlord said we had to leave because his son

"My dad . . . left Japan at the age of 14. . . . I remember, in his lifetime, I only saw him cry three times. Once was on the seventh of December, because he couldn't understand why the land of his birth had attacked the land of his heart."

—*Norman Mineta, the son of a Japanese immigrant to the United States. Mineta later became the United States Secretary of Transportation.*[2]

▲ **Norman Mineta remembered growing up with his father, who immigrated to the United States from Japan.**

was coming home," she recalled.[3] The son was fighting against Japan in the war. He did not want any Japanese Americans in the building. Without warning, Tokuno and her sister needed to look for a new home.

Many other Japanese Americans faced similar problems. After the Pearl Harbor attack, some were fired from their jobs. Others lost their homes. For many Japanese Americans, a new challenge lay ahead.

Chapter 2

EXECUTIVE ORDER 9066

B y the 1940s, Japanese Americans lived in different communities across the nation. Issei and Nisei often had important jobs. Yet, after the United States declared war on Japan, many lost friends. In stores, some clerks helped Japanese Americans only after they had helped all of the other customers. Officials with the

Federal Bureau of Investigation (FBI) searched the homes of Japanese Americans. The FBI took cameras, radios, and other items. Some Issei hid or destroyed their Japanese books and clothes. "Neighbors were watching us and reporting to the FBI that we were having secret meetings," said Mary Tsukamoto. "We would be reported, and the police would come."[4]

Some authorities worried that Japanese Americans could help Japan attack the United States. Government officials urged the president to take action. On February 19, 1942, President Roosevelt signed Executive Order 9066. An executive order is a rule created by the president. It is similar to a law. Executive Order 9066 allowed the United States War Department to create "military areas." Authorities could force any person to leave these areas. They used the order to force Japanese Americans to leave their homes.

Under Order 9066, an agency called the War Relocation Authority (WRA) set up large military areas. The areas included all of California and parts of Washington, Arizona, and Oregon. These were states with large Japanese-American populations. Later, the WRA added military areas in other regions. The agency banned Japanese and Japanese-American people

> "There was no other choice but to obey the orders. We were given seven days to pack and sell or store our household belongings, our car, truck, and everything used to run the farm. In one week we had to leave, ready or not. On evacuation we could take only what we could carry, which was very little."
>
> —Gloria Morita[5]

from these areas. A much smaller number of German Americans and Italian Americans also were banned from the areas.

Japanese Americans in these areas had to **evacuate** their homes. At first, officials encouraged them to move. Some families quickly packed up their belongings and moved to other states. But thousands of people stayed. Soon, the WRA began forcing them to leave. The agency loaded Japanese Americans onto hot, crowded trains. The trains brought them to internment camps. The U.S. government also took control of businesses, banks, and newspapers owned by Japanese Americans. Authorities closed many Japanese language schools.

In 1942, President Franklin Roosevelt signed ▶ Executive Order 9066.

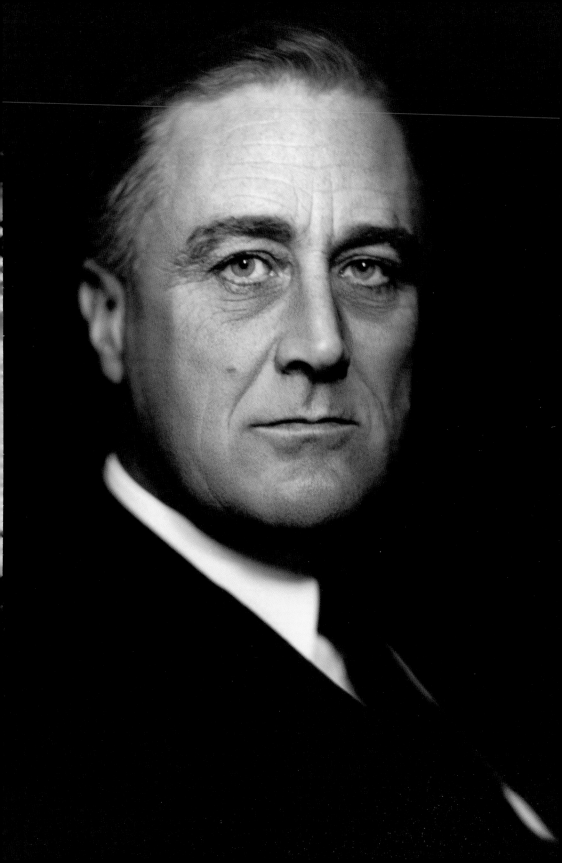

▲ **A Japanese-American family prepared to leave for an internment camp.**

In March 1942, the WRA tacked up posters in cities on the West Coast. The posters warned all Japanese Americans to evacuate by April 7, 1942. Trains would take them to internment camps. "Somebody from Seattle came over," explained Paul Ohtaki. His family lived in nearby Bainbridge Island, Washington. He was 17 years old when they were forced to move. "He said, 'You guys are going to have to leave in a week.' Then, a few days later, the army came over and they tacked up these little posters."[6] The posters ordered Japanese Americans to leave their homes. Soon, the Ohtakis were taken to Manzanar, an internment camp in California.

Some families had only 24 hours to prepare for this move. Each person was allowed to bring only two suitcases of belongings. Families rushed to sell refrigerators, new furniture, and even cars that they could not take with them. Crafty salespeople bought these goods from the families for very low prices. Then, Japanese Americans tearfully said goodbye to their homes and neighbors. After they had left, some towns were nearly abandoned, filled with rows of empty houses.

Dolores Silva lived in a neighborhood with families from Japan and Portugal. She recalled saying goodbye to her Japanese-American friends. "These students that we were going to school with, they were like our family," Silva said. "All of a sudden [the WRA] said you have to leave within three days. And it was a terrible shock to us. I just felt so bad. We had our arms around each other that last day of school and we were all crying. Because we didn't want them to go. It was not fair."[7]

Chapter 3

MOVING TO THE INTERNMENT CAMPS

Most Issei and Nisei people obeyed the government's orders. But some Japanese Americans defended their right to stay in their homes. One man, Fred Korematsu, used disguises to make himself look less Japanese. He changed the name on his identity card to Clyde Sarah. On May 30, 1942, Korematsu was caught and sent to jail.

The Japanese American Citizens League (JACL) encouraged people to follow the government's instructions. They wanted to show their loyalty to the United States. "JACL decided in the beginning of the war to cooperate with the U.S. government," said Norman Mineta. "That would prove our American **patriotism**."[8] Mineta's brother-in-law was a member of JACL.

At the time, Mineta was 11 years old. His experience going to an internment camp was different from his parents' experience. Mineta remembered thinking, "Wow, I am going to be on an overnight train ride!"[9] He brought a baseball with a bat and glove with him. On the train, Mineta thought about playing with other children at the camp. But when he looked at his parents, he saw that his father was crying.

Hundreds of boys and girls were traveling to the camp. For some of the children, living so close to their friends was exciting. Others were very sad to leave their homes. Mary Tsukamoto remembered arriving at the internment camp. "We saw all these people behind the fence, looking out, hanging onto the wire," she said. "When the gates were shut, we knew that we had lost something very precious, that we were no longer free."[10]

The journey to the internment camp was often long. Mineta spent hours on the train. His home was in San Jose, California. The camp was in Heart Mountain, Wyoming, more than 1,100 miles (1,770 km) away. Heart Mountain was one of 10 internment camps in the United States. At one time, it housed 10,767 people. In all, more than 112,000 Japanese Americans were sent to the camps. More than half of them were American citizens.

Guards watched people in internment camps from ▶ high towers.

Chapter 4

LIFE IN THE CAMPS

Families found the camps very different from their homes. Paul Ohtaki was from Bainbridge, Washington. Spring had just begun in his hometown. Ohtaki knew that the grass was turning green in Bainbridge. The strawberries were ripening. But the ground was dry and dusty at the Manzanar internment camp. Manzanar was in a desert area of California. The weather was harsh. Temperatures were high. The landscape was nothing more than sand for miles.

The camps were built to house people. But they were not very comfortable. The camps had been constructed quickly. Several thousand **barracks** were built in a few months. The barracks did not have bathrooms, kitchens, or even running water. Camps had few doctors. As a result, people received little medical care. They did not know when they would be released. Families ate meals in a mess hall similar to a cafeteria. They had little privacy. Barbed-wire fences surrounded the camp. Armed guards, or sentries, watched the **internees** from giant watchtowers. The guards reminded the internees that they were not free.

Life was difficult for the internees. They had lost their homes and communities. Many had to work in the camps as farmers, construction workers, or janitors for little pay. Often, they had to

"I do not like the idea of loyal citizens, whatever their race or color, being kept in relocation centers any longer than need be."

—*U.S. Secretary of the Interior Harold Ickes*[11]

21

stand in long lines for meals. Despite their hardships, many made do with what they had. Internees repeated the words *shikata ga nai*, "It cannot be helped." They used scrap lumber to put up extra walls for privacy. Some planted flower gardens and built Japanese rock gardens. They bought or made colorful curtains.

The internees still deeply missed their homes. But many were proud of their work. "When we entered camp, it was a **barren** desert," said an internee. "When we left camp, it was a garden that had been built up without tools. It was green around the camp."[12]

Many internees worked on farms at ▶
Manzanar internment camp.

Chapter 5

THE END OF INTERNMENT

While Japanese-American families stayed in internment camps, the war continued. U.S. forces were fighting in Europe, Asia, and Africa. Millions of Americans were serving in the military.

When internment began, Japanese Americans were not allowed to serve in the armed forces. Some internees wanted to join. Many hoped to show their patriotism that way. Others simply wanted to leave the camps. They asked government officials to let them serve.

Mike Masaoka's parents were Japanese immigrants. Because he lived in Salt Lake City, Utah, he was not interned during the war. A talented speaker, Masaoka wanted to persuade people that Japanese Americans were loyal citizens. He joined the Japanese American Citizens League in 1938. By 1941, he was the national secretary of the organization. Masaoka harshly criticized Japanese Americans who disobeyed internment orders. He believed that Issei and Nisei could show patriotism by obeying laws. Though some disagreed, Masaoka's efforts had some success.

Masaoka worked hard to convince authorities to accept Nisei citizens into the military. In 1943, the government agreed. President Roosevelt announced a new **battalion** of Japanese-American soldiers. Nearly 1,500 interned Japanese Americans joined the 442nd Regimental Combat Team. They left the camps for military service in Europe.

"We all had the idea of proving that we were loyal Americans," said Tim Tokuno. He served on the combat team.

▲ **Japanese-American soldiers fought for the United States in World War II.**

"Everything was 'go, go, go forward, go forward.' And . . . we never retreated. We never took a backward step. Always forward."[13] Military leaders praised the battalion. The soldiers won many military honors. One internee won a Medal of Honor—the highest military honor in the United States.

Japanese Americans also helped the U.S. war effort in other ways. Some translated documents about the Japanese forces' military plans. Others served as medics or nurses.

Meanwhile, authorities debated whether to continue interning Japanese Americans. The camps were built to prevent disloyalty. But there were no signs that Japanese Americans were helping enemy forces. Many people believed that it wasn't right to lock up people who had done nothing wrong. In 1944, the U.S. Supreme Court heard two cases about the internment camps. *Korematsu v. United States* was the case of Japanese-American Fred Korematsu. He had refused to go to an internment camp. The justices ruled that Korematsu could be forced to go to the camp. But in another case, *Ex parte Endo*, justices ruled that the government could not **detain** internees without a reason. Starting in January 1945, internees were allowed to leave the camps. Many had been interned for three years. In 1945, the war ended, but some internees were still living in the camps. By 1946, all of the camps had closed.

After they had been freed, Japanese Americans

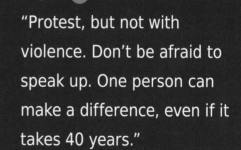

"Protest, but not with violence. Don't be afraid to speak up. One person can make a difference, even if it takes 40 years."

—*Fred Korematsu*[14]

faced hardships. They returned to their homes with their suitcases, a bus ticket, and $20. Many had lost their jobs and struggled to find work. Families found others living in their homes. Some Japanese-American households had been burglarized or vandalized. "It was our house, but it wasn't anymore," said Aya Nakamura.[15]

Many internees started difficult new lives in different parts of the country. Slowly, they found new jobs and communities. "It hurt not being able to return home, but moving into a new home helped me," said Nakamura. "I think it helped me to bury the past a little."[16]

As time passed, more Americans recognized that internment took away people's freedom. In 1948, the U.S. government paid internees a total of $37 million for their lost property. The money helped some families buy new homes. Still, many never received any money. In later decades, internees spoke publicly about their

"Not only was the evacuation wrong, but Japanese Americans were and are loyal Americans."

—President Gerald Ford on February 19, 1976, exactly 34 years after President Roosevelt signed Executive Order 9066[17]

experiences. In 1988, officials gave $20,000 to each surviving internee. The government also made an official apology to survivors of the internment camps.

▲ In 1998, President Bill Clinton awarded Fred Korematsu the Presidential Medal of Freedom for his efforts to fight internment.

GLOSSARY

allies (AL-eyes): Allies are countries that join together to help one another. Japan, Germany, and Italy were allies.

barracks (BA-rucks): Barracks are buildings for large numbers of people. Japanese Americans lived in barracks at the internment camps.

barren (BA-ren): Barren land has few plants. Some of the internment camps were on dry, barren land.

battalion (ba-TAL-yun): A battalion is a large group of soldiers. The 442nd Regimental Combat Team was a battalion of Japanese-American soldiers in World War II.

detain (dee-TAYN): To detain a person is to prevent them from leaving a place. The U.S. Supreme Court ruled that the government could not detain Japanese Americans.

ethnicity (eth-NISS-i-tee): People with a certain ethnicity are originally from the same nation or culture. Japanese Americans shared an ethnicity.

evacuate (ee-VAK-you-ayt): When people evacuate an area, they leave. During World War II, many Japanese Americans had to evacuate their homes.

internees (in-TURN-eez): Internees are people who are kept in an internment camp. Some internees planted flowers at the camps.

patriotism (PAY-tree-uh-ti-zum): Patriotism is a feeling of pride for a person's country. Many Japanese Americans wanted to show their patriotism for the United States.

prejudice (PREH-juh-diss): Prejudice is an unfair way of thinking about a group of people. Japanese Americans often faced prejudice.

SOURCE NOTES

1. "A Necessary War." *Ken Burns: The War.* PBS, 2007. Web. 26 May 2015.

2. "Interview: Norman Mineta." *Academy of Achievement.* American Academy of Achievement, 23 April 2008. Web. 7 August 2015.

3. "A Necessary War." 2007.

4. Ann Heinrichs. *The Japanese American Internment: Innocence, Guilt, and Wartime Justice.* New York: Cavendish Square, 2010. Print. 29.

5. "Gloria Morita Recalls Executive Order 9066." *PANA Institute Voices.* PANA Institute, 8 April 2008. Web. 26 May 2015.

6. "Japanese Americans Interned During World War II – Paul Ohtaki." *Telling Their Stories: Oral History Archives Project.* The Urban School of San Francisco, 31 January 2008. Web. 26 May 2015.

7. "Japanese Americans." *The War: At Home – Civil Rights.* PBS, n.d. Web. 26 May 2015.

8. "Mineta, Norman Y., (1931–)." *Biography.* Biographical Directory of the United States Congress, n.d. Web. 26 May 2015.

9. "Interview: Norman Mineta." 23 April 2008.

10. "Daily Life in the Internment Camps." *OurStory.* Smithsonian National Museum of American History, n.d. Web. 26 May 2015.

11. Jeff Carroll. *Sam Rice: A Biography of the Washington Senators Hall of Famer.* Cooperstown, NY: McFarland Press, 2008. Print. 193.

12. Commission on Wartime Relocation and Internment of Civilians. *Personal Justice Denied.* Washington, DC: University of Washington Press, 1997. Print. 161.

13. "Tim Tokuno." *Witnesses.* PBS, 2007. Web. 26 May 2015.

14. "Honoring a Japanese-American Who Fought Against Internment Camps." *All Things Considered.* National Public Radio, 30 January 2014. Web. 26 May 2015.

15-16. Robin Roth. "Life After Japanese Internment Camps." *History of Japanese Internment Camps.* n.p., 27 November 2008. Web. 26 May 2015.

17. "Daily Life in the Internment Camps." n.d.

TO LEARN MORE

Books

Houston, Jeanne W., and James D. Houston. *Farewell to Manzanar*. New York: Random House, 2012.

Perl, Lila. *Behind Barbed Wire: The Story of Japanese Internment during World War II*. New York: Cavendish Square, 2012.

Sandler, Martin W. *Imprisoned: The Betrayal of Japanese Americans during World War II*. London: Walker, 2013.

Web Sites

Visit our Web site for links about Japanese-American internment during World War II: childsworld.com/links

Note to Parents, Teachers, and Librarians: We routinely verify our Web links to make sure they are safe and active sites. So encourage your readers to check them out!

INDEX